Bananas i

Helen

and
Morag Styles

Illustrated by
Jane Gedye

CAMBRIDGE
UNIVERSITY PRESS

PUBLISHED BY THE PRESS SYNDICATE OF THE UNIVERSITY OF CAMBRIDGE
The Pitt Building, Trumpington Street, Cambridge CB2 1RP, United Kingdom

CAMBRIDGE UNIVERSITY PRESS
The Edinburgh Building, Cambridge CB2 2RU, United Kingdom
40 West 20th Street, New York, NY 10011-4211, USA
10 Stamford Road, Oakleigh, Melbourne 3166, Australia

This selection © Cambridge University Press 1991
Illustrations © Jayne Gedye 1991
Cover illustration © Sue Hellard 1998
Project editor: Claire Llewellyn

First published 1991
Reprinted 1998 (twice)

Printed in the United Kingdom at the University Press, Cambridge

Typeset in Photina

A catalogue record for this book is available from the British Library

ISBN 0 521 39948 3 paperback

Acknowledgements

'Bananas in Pyjamas' reproduced by permission of Carey Blyton, composer/author; 'Jim-Jam Pyjamas'
from *Jim-Jam Pyjamas* by Gina Wilson, Jonathan Cape Ltd, 1990, © Gina Wilson 1990; 'Ode to the
Queen on her Jubilee' from *Startling Verse for All the Family* by Spike Milligan (Puffin Books), © Spike
Milligan Productions; 'Humpty Dumpty' and 'This Little Pig' from *Hairy Tales and Nursery Crimes* ©
Michael Rosen, 1986, first published by André Deutsch Children's Books, an imprint of Scholastic Ltd.;
'Dis Lickle Pig' from *Jamaica Maddah Goose*, compiled by Donald Robertson, edited by Louise Bennett,
reprinted with the permission of The Association of Friends of The Edna Manley For The Visual Arts
(formerly The Jamaica School of Art); 'Back Yard, July Night' © 1969 by William Cole; 'Pet Food' by
Terry Jones, reprinted by permission of Pavilion Books from *The Curse of the Vampire's Socks* by Terry
Jones; 'Nature Poem' © Adrian Mitchell. Available in *Balloon Lagoon and the Magic of Islands Poetry*
(Orchard Books, 1997). Reprinted by permission of The Peters Fraser and Dunlop Group Limited on
behalf of Adrian Mitchell; 'The One who does not Love Me' (trad. Yoruba) from *Yoruba
Poetry*, Cambridge University Press 1970; 'Black Dot' copyright © Libby Houston 1993 from *All
Change*, Oxford University Press, reprinted by permission of the author; 'P's and 'Q's from *Nailing the
Shadow* by Roger McGough. Reprinted by permission of The Peters Fraser and Dunlop Group Ltd on
behalf of Roger McGough © 1987; 'To Amuse Emus' from *An Imaginary Menagerie* by Roger McGough.
Reprinted by permission of The Peters Fraser and Dunlop Group Limited on behalf of Roger McGough
© 1988; 'Ruthless Rhyme Five' by Harry Graham from *Most Ruthless Rhymes for Heartless Homes*,
Edward Arnold; 'Short Sharp Shock' is taken from *There's an Awful Lot of Weirdos in our Neighbourhood*
© 1987 Colin McNaughton, first published in the UK by Walker Books Ltd; 'The Gentle Giant' by
Dennis Lee, from *Jelly Belly*, published by Macmillan of Canada, © Dennis Lee; 'Have You Seen the
Hidebehind' © Michael Rosen, 1974, from *Mind Your Own Business*, first published by André Deutsch
Children's Books, an imprint of Scholastic Ltd.; 'Dragon Night' copyright © 1980 by Jane Yolen.
Reprinted by permission of Curtis Brown, Ltd.; 'Sweet Dreams' reprinted by permission of Curtis
Brown, Ltd. Copyright © 1961 by Ogden Nash.

Every effort has been made to reach copyright holders; the publishers would be glad to hear from
anyone whose rights they have unknowingly infringed.

Contents

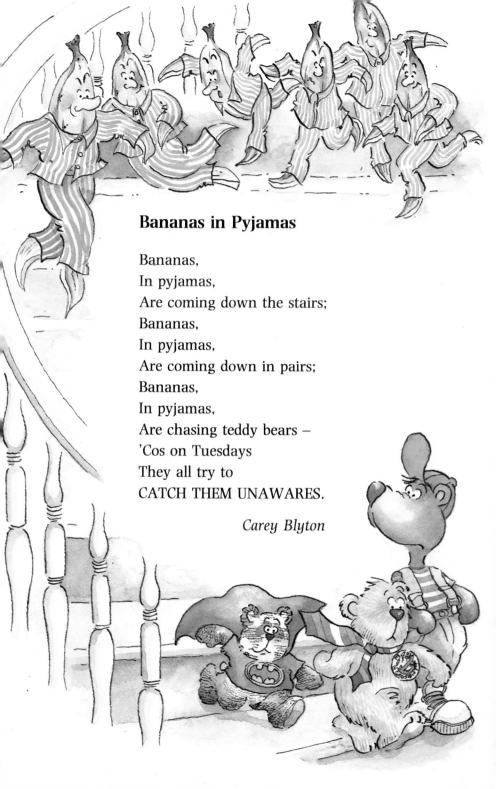

Bananas in Pyjamas

Bananas,
In pyjamas,
Are coming down the stairs;
Bananas,
In pyjamas,
Are coming down in pairs;
Bananas,
In pyjamas,
Are chasing teddy bears –
'Cos on Tuesdays
They all try to
CATCH THEM UNAWARES.

Carey Blyton

Jim-Jam Pyjamas

He wears striped jim-jam pyjamas,
You never saw jim-jams like those –
A fine-fitting, stretchy, fur cat-suit,
Skin-tight from his head to his toes.

He wears striped jim-jam pyjamas,
Black and yellow and dashingly gay;
He makes certain that everyone sees them
By keeping them on all the day.

He wears striped jim-jam pyjamas,
He walks with a smug-pussy stride;
There's no hiding his pride in his jim-jams
With their zig-zaggy lines down each side.

He wears striped jim-jam pyjamas
And pauses at times to display
The effect as he flexes his torso –
Then he fancies he hears people say:

'I wish I had jim-jam pyjamas!
I wish I were feline and slim!
Oh, look at that brave Bengal tiger!
Oh, how I should love to be him!'

Gina Wilson

Ode to the Queen on Her Jubilee

Sound the trumpet,
Bang the drum,
Shake the tambourine
Because this year is Jubilee
But only for the Quine.
So glory, glory,
Gloria!
Regina gloriana!
You are the apple
Of my eye
Let me be your banana!

Spike Milligan

Humpty Dumpty

Humpty Dumpty sat on a wall,
Eating black bananas.
Where do you think he put the skins?
Down the King's pyjamas.

Anon

Humpty Dumpty

Humpty Dumpty sat on the wall,
Humpty Dumpty had a great fall;
All the King's horses and all the King's men
Trod on him.

Michael Rosen

Piggy on the Railway

Piggy on the railway
Picking up stones,
Along came an engine
And broke Piggy's bones.

'Oy,' said Piggy,
'That's not fair.'
'Pooh,' said the engine driver,
'I don't care.'

Anon

Dis Lickle Pig

Dis lickle pig go a markit,
  Dis lickle pig tan a yaad,
Dis lickle pig nyam curry goat,
  Dis lickle pig got nun,
Dis lickle pig holla, 'Wahi, wahi, wahi!'
  All de way a im yaad.

From *Jamaica Maddah Goose*

This Little Pig

This little pig went to market,
This little pig ate some ants,
This little pig went to Sainsbury's,
This little pig went up in a lift,
And this little pig
Went wee wee wee wee wee wee,
Oh no, I've wet my pants.

Michael Rosen

The Man in the Wilderness

The man in the wilderness asked of me,
How many strawberries grow in the sea?
I answered him as I thought good
As many red herrings as grow in a wood.

Anon

There was an Old Man in a Tree

There was an old man in a tree,
Whose whiskers were lovely to see;
But the birds of the air pluck'd them perfectly bare,
To make themselves nests in that tree.

Edward Lear

Twinkle, Twinkle, Little Bat!

Twinkle, twinkle, little bat!
How I wonder what you're at!
Up above the world you fly,
Like a tea-tray in the sky.

Lewis Carroll

Back Yard, July Night

Firefly, airplane, satellite, star –
How I wonder which you are.

William Cole

RACT FROM **The Star**

our bright and tiny spark
ts the traveller in the dark,
ugh I know not what you are,
nkle, twinkle, little star.

Jane Taylor

Pet Food

What do you get, Jude,
When you eat Pet Food?

Hamsterburgers,
Poodle Pies,
Goldfish Fingers,
Canary Fries.

Budgie Bangers,
Dachshunds and Mash,
Pickled Parrots,
Corned Cat Hash.

Gerbils on Toast,
Tortoise Teas,
Horse-in-a-basket,
Mice and Peas.

That's what you get, Jude,
When you eat Pet Food!

Terry Jones

Nature Poem

Skylark, what prompts your silver song
To fountain up and down the sky?

> Beetles roast
> With fleas on toast
> And earthworm pie.

Adrian Mitchell

The Squirrel

The winds they did blow,
The leaves they did wag;
Along came a beggar boy
And put me in a bag.

He took me to London,
A lady did me buy,
Put me in a silver cage
And hung me up on high.

With apples by the fire
And nuts for to crack,
Besides a little feather bed
To rest my little back.

Anon

Rope Rhyme

Get set, ready now, jump right in
Bounce and kick and giggle and spin
Listen to the rope when it hits the ground
Listen to that clappedy-slappedy sound
Jump right up when it tells you to
Come back down whatever you do
Count to a hundred, count by ten
Start to count all over again

That's what jumping is all about
Get set, ready now,

20

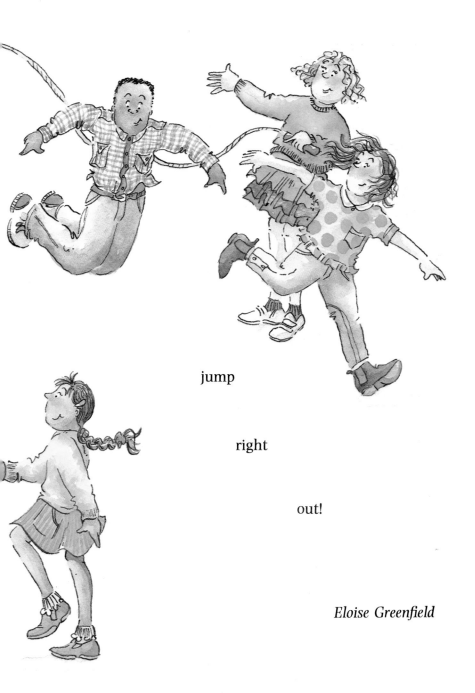

jump

right

out!

Eloise Greenfield

Jumping Joan

Here am I,

Little Jumping Joan;

When nobody's with me

I'm all alone.

Anon

The One who does not Love Me

The one who does not love me,
He will become a frog
And he will jump jump jump away:
He will become a monkey with one leg
And he will hop hop hop away.

Traditional, Nigeria

23

Black Dot

a black dot
a jelly tot

a scum-nail
a jiggle-tail

a cool kicker
a sitting slicker

a panting puffer
a fly-snuffer

a high hopper
a belly-flopper

a catalogue
  to make me

                    frog

Libby Houston

The Frog

What a wonderful bird the frog are –
When he sit, he stand almost;
When he hop, he fly almost.
He ain't got no sense hardly;
He ain't got no tail hardly either.
When he sit, he sit on what he ain't got – almost.

Anon

P's and Q's

I quite often confuse
My quees and my poos.

Roger McGough

To Amuse Emus

To amuse
   emus
on warm summer nights

   Kiwis
do wiwis
from spectacular heights.

Roger McGough

Ruthless Rhyme Five

Father heard his children scream,
So he threw them in the stream,
Saying, as he dropped the third,
'Children should be seen not heard.'

Harry Graham

Short Sharp Shock

If your children are ever unruly,
(Of course this might never happen),
Just tell them to kindly behave themselves,
Then reach over quickly and slap 'em!

Colin McNaughton

The Gentle Giant

Every night
At twelve o'clock,
The gentle giant
Takes a walk;
With a cry cried high
And a call called low,
The gentle giant
Walks below.

And as he walks,
He cries, he calls:

'Bad men, boogie men,
Bully men, shoo!
No one in the neighbourhood
Is scared of you.
The children are asleep,
And the parents are too:
Bad men, boogie men,
Bully men, shoo!'

Dennis Lee

29

Have You Seen the Hidebehind?

Have you seen the Hidebehind?
I don't think you will, mind you,
because as you're running through the dark
the Hidebehind's behind you.

Michael Rosen

Dragon Night

Little flame mouths,
Cool your tongues.
Dreamtime starts,
My furnace lungs.

Rest your wings now,
Little flappers,
Cave mouth calls
To dragon nappers.

Night is coming,
Bank your fire.
Time for dragons
To retire.

Hiss.
Hush.
Sleep.

Jane Yolen

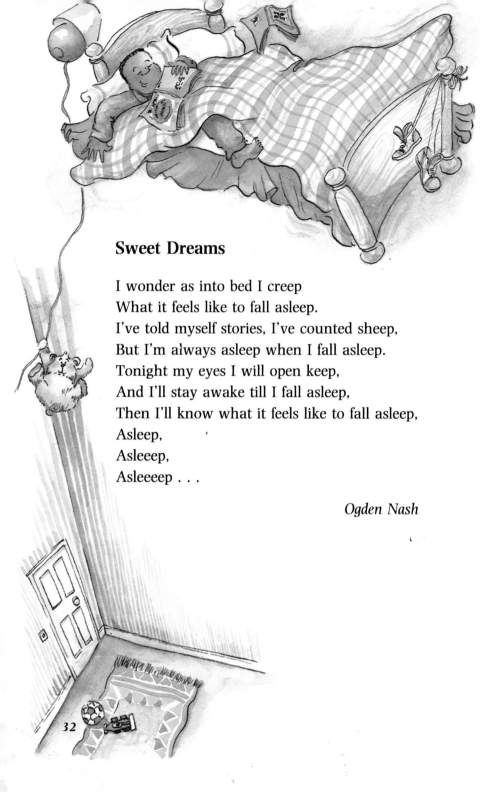

Sweet Dreams

I wonder as into bed I creep
What it feels like to fall asleep.
I've told myself stories, I've counted sheep,
But I'm always asleep when I fall asleep.
Tonight my eyes I will open keep,
And I'll stay awake till I fall asleep,
Then I'll know what it feels like to fall asleep,
Asleep,
Asleeep,
Asleeeep . . .

Ogden Nash